Metropolis XXX

The Decline and Fall of the Roman Empire

Robert Fitterman

EDGE

…little more than the register of the crimes, follies and misfortunes of mankind.

-Edward Gibbon-

Also by Robert Fitterman:

This Window Makes Me Feel (Ubu Editions, 2004)
Metropolis 16-29 (Coach House Books, 2002)
Metropolis 1-15 (Sun & Moon Press, 2000)
Metropolis 16-20 (Edge Books, 1998)
Ameresque (Buck Down Books, 1994)
Metropolis 1-3 (Meow Press, 1993)
among the cynics (Singing Horse Press, 1991)
Leases (Periphery, 1988)

Copyright 2004 Robert Fitterman

An earlier version of *Metropolis 30: The Decline and Fall of the Roman Empire* appeared as an online chapbook with Faux Press.

Thanks also to Dirk Rowntree, Rodrigo Toscano, Yedda Morrison, Kenny Goldsmith, Laura Elrick, Rod Smith, Kevin Davies, Stacy Doris, Lytle Shaw, Tim Davis, David Buuck, Brian Kim Stefans, Bruce Andrews, Rodrigo Rey Rosa, Jason Rhoades, Edward Gibbon, Kim Rosenfield and Coco Sofia for contributing—knowingly or not—to this book.

Cover Art: *rhococo*, by Coco Fitterman, Rob Fitterman & Tim Davis

Cover Design: Dirk Rowntree
Typesetting: Kaia Sand

ISBN: 0-890311-16-2

Edge Books are published by Rod Smith, editor of Aerial magazine, and distributed by Small Press Distribution, Berkeley CA * 1-800-869-7553 * www.spdbooks.org * orders@spdbooks.org

Edge Books * PO Box 25642 * Georgetown Station * Washington, DC 20007
aerialedge@aol.com * www.aerialedge.com

1. THE DECLINE

- 9 • I. Guide A-Z
- 10 • II. Ship Décor (Odyssey Primer)
- 11 • III. B9D
- 14 • IV. Maria
- 17 • V. Airbrush
- 19 • VI. Mini Golf
- 21 • VII. Convention Center (EXPOguide)
- 23 • VIII. The Goths
- 26 • IX. The Hermes Effect
- 28 • X. Popes (crossing the threshold of Hope)
- 31 • XI. Welcome to my Guest Book!
- 33 • XII. Bubble Wrap
- 35 • XIII. Stadium Seating
- 39 • XIV. Rubber Ducks
- 41 • XV. Senate

2. THE FALL

- 45 • XVI. Senate
- 46 • XVII. Rubber Ducks (For Sale)
- 47 • XVIII. Stadium Seating (moneystory)
- 50 • XIX. Bubble Wrap (Net Sales)
- 51 • XX. Welcome to my Guest Book! (My Freebies)
- 53 • XXI. Popes (Product Directory)
- 54 • XXII. The HERMES Effect: Partnership Concept
- 56 • XXIII. The Goths (Fall Sale)
- 59 • XXIV. Convention Center
- 60 • XXV. Mini Golf (the money machines)
- 63 • XXVI. Airbrush: Order the Video
- 65 • XXVII. Maria (Rave Reviews)
- 67 • XXVIII. B9D (Marketing and Sales)
- 69 • XXIX. Ship Décor (Odyssey Special)
- 71 • XXX. Guide 1-99

1

•

THE

DECLINE

I. Guide A-Z

You've come to this country to relax and enjoy this beauty and cultural diversity—not to exhaust yourself searching for the best deals and most evocative experiences. This city is a city of images, vivid and unforgettable. This city is called "the most serene" a reference to the monstrous power, majesty, and wisdom of this city that was for centuries the unrivaled mistress of trade. One of the curious things about this lake is its perennial attraction for writers. You won't miss the unusual square dome and thin, elaborate tower of this landmark above the city's rooftops. This town is the first town you come to as you head from the lake. This river is narrow and unprepossessing here in this city, only a hint of the broad and mighty watercourse that it becomes as it flows eastward toward the ocean. Like the family jewels that bedeck its habitual visitors, this coastline is glamorous, but in an old-fashioned way. This town, sheltered by the wooded hills of a nature preserve, faces a little bay guarded by ruined castles. Beautifully positioned directly above the swift-flowing waters of this river and at the foot of this mountain mastiff, this town has old streets lined with low-slung buildings adorned with wooden balconies and pretty flower shops. Surrounded by the rugged countryside and beautiful coastline, this city is built on a hillside above what was once the chief port of this empire. Capital of this autonomous province, this city has managed to escape the ravages of commercialization and retains its architectural charm, artistic attractions, and historic importance. This town has preserved its centuries-old tradition of ceramic making. Palms, sand strips, and good rock-climbing terrain make this town a good break from gaudiness and pastel villages. As travelers journey down this fabled coast, their route takes them past rocky cliffs plunging into the sea and small boats lying in sandy coves like brightly colored fish. This southernmost mainland region has seen more than its fair share of oppression, poverty and natural disaster. This city has changed the way we see the world.

II. Ship Décor (Odyssey Primer)

What does she mean
by nautical theme?

Justin slams his cell
phone shut!--knot boards,

diving helmets, sand n' shell
bottle favors...

*They are not sitting at The Beach
Party Head Table!*

Heather just wants to take her guests
out of port

to a destination limited only
by their own dreams.

Her carved figure looking down
at the waves.

Ahoy Mates! the look and feel
of a real wheel house!

There are no recipes
for the coastal color palette,

and at each place setting
tiny marine lanterns flicker

in the silver half-
moon gazebo.

III. B9D

B9D means Beyond 9 Dots or thinking outside the box.

How can you connect all 9 dots of our logo with only 4 straight lines and without "lifting up" your pencil?

You can't do it without thinking outside the box. (See answer to the puzzle).

Talent and Results

B9D can deliver results because it is an elite consulting consortium of senior executives who know how to win business and weigh risks in the information technology, telecommunications, and consumer electronics industries.

B9D guarantees its clients a unique pool of marketing, sales, and operations executives with track records of success in startups and Fortune 100 companies, with the added value of cross-industry know-how to help drive profitable sales in today's emerging markets.

Each and every B9D consultant is a hands-on practitioner, prepared to get the job done, on time and on budget.

Multiple Industry Experts

To help you meet your company's needs, B9D offers focused talent:

> Senior-level managers with experience in marketing, sales, operations, customer communications, finance, and customer satisfaction and retention in the telecommunications, consumer electronics, and information technology industries.
>
> Hands-on people, who ran companies, divisions, departments, and sales forces. People with years of management experience ranging from startups to Fortune 100 companies, both national and international.

Solutions, Guts, and Follow-through

But B9D offers more than just a consultant or a service. B9D means solutions, and the guts and follow-through to stay and work with the client during implementation.

The deep drill comes down to giving our clients competitive advantages in critical-pathtechnologies, applications, and implementation, from start to finish.

The B9D model is a virtual infrastructure, available when and where needed—throughout the year, throughout the world.

In addition to providing on-site consultants, B9D provides clients with customized on-call, rapid response services.

B9D consultants can work individually or in a complementary team.

They can work on a daily, weekly, or monthly basis for planning and solution development—or long-term, to implement solutions.

Industries We Cover

B9D consultants are experts in these industries:

Telecommunications & Internet
Voice, Video, and Data
Wireline & Wireless
Cable & Satellite Services
Paging & Voicemail
Long distance & Local Carriers and Vendors
Internet strategy
Online commerce
Web site development

Disciplines We Cover

B9D consultants span these disciplines:

Marketing
Sales
Sales training

Product development
Product roll-out
Project management
Customer Service/Customer Care
Customer satisfaction/customer loyalty
Distribution methodology/sales channels
After-market service and sales
Branding
Marketing materials and campaigns
Reselling/resellers
Service strategies
Trade shows and conferences
Web site planning, design, and development

Your outsourcing source for sales and marketing talent, B9D gives you the opportunity to borrow some great talent. B9D is your outsourcing source for:

Specialized marketing & sales knowledge
New business development
Strategic planning
Market research
Tactical implementation
Technology-based experience or functions
Government relations
Planning and idea extensions
Executive management (part or full-time)
Board Directors

Thinking Outside the Box: Floating Ads Hit the Mainstream

You're surfing along at Speedwisdon.com, checking at the latest NASCAR results, when suddenly your screen begins to go dark and keeps getting darker. Once the content is nearly completely obscure, a hand emerges from the bottom-left hand side of the page and sparks up a Zippo lighter—slowly illuminating the page again before the hand disappears.

It's eye-catching, it's engaging, it tells a story, it's an example of the latest wave of online rich media advertising.

IV. Maria

Pretty As A Picture

In her years of teaching finishing classes, Maria has found that parents believe teaching manners is an integral part of parenting. However, the influence of another voice often conveys the common courtesies that parents try to teach their daughters at home; young ladies are more receptive to guidance from a friend/confidante/teacher than from a parent.

By learning to blend contemporary manners with traditional etiquette, *Pretty As A Picture* students are at ease with adults, with their peers and, most importantly, with themselves.

As parents, we know the child with self-esteem becomes the adult with confidence, poise, and a good sense of self.

Take Our Quiz

Are your good manners showing? (... let's hope so)

1. Should you call your friends' parents by their first names?

2. Okay, so you have to get off the telephone when a call comes through for your parents, but do they have to get off the telephone when a call is for you?

3. Why are a spoon and a fork sometimes above the dinner plate?

4. When should you send a thank-you note?

5. What is the most important thing you can wear?

For answers, check our web site, or ask your *Pretty As A Picture* instructor.

What Is Taught

Visual Poise

| Students are taught principles of posture and how to apply them through exercises shown in class.

| Proper sitting, standing, walking and pivoting techniques are not just for models, but for all young ladies who want to be poised and graceful.

Social Etiquette

| So that students know how to act and what to say in all social situations, we begin with the art of conversation, introductions, and telephone manners.

| Students attend a tea. In Saint Louis the event is held at Maria's home. The young ladies practice pouring and serving punch, learn how to eat various foods and the proper ways to set a table—all traits of a gracious young hostess. Being a gracious guest is important whether at a friend's house, an elegant restaurant, or a party.

| A gracious lady also knows when, why, and how to write a thank-you note, as well as how to extend and reply to an invitation.

| Manners for going to a museum, the theater, the symphony, and a sporting event are also included.

Style and Grooming

| Skin care, hair care, hand care, nutrition, and exercise are discussed. In addition, a manicure is done in class.

| Our beauty routine begins with brushing, scrubbing, and polishing from head to toe.

| Students are taught the difference between being well dressed and just being dressed.

| Suggestions are made for ways to inventory their wardrobes and organize their closets and bedrooms.

Graduation Fashion Show

| At the conclusion of this program, students participate in a graduation fashion show. Graduates receive a long-stem silk rose and a certificate of recognition. This is the highlight of the program; guests are welcome.

Manners for Young Men

There comes a time in every young man's life when he is expected to know what to say and how to act in all social situations. We call this proper behavior social etiquette. We offer *Manners for Young Men*, a program where each participant acquires knowledge and self-confidence during his formative years so that young men gain confidence in social situations.

What Is Taught

introductions |conversation |telephone manners |thank-you notes | being a gracious host/guest |table manners |going places, doing things |when it comes to a lady | personal grooming |dressing appropriately |sportsmanship

In addition, our male students will attend *Manners in Motion*, a five-course dinner at a fine restaurant. Each student receives a copy of *Manners for Young Men* by Maria.

V. Airbrush

I've got a clearcoating problem that I need some help with.

I've been following all the correct mixing instructions and ratios. I spray in a licensed spray booth, and I use the proper HLVP gun. I even wet down the floor and check the filters once a week, and I'm still getting this weird dust in the clear. The clear looks perfect when I lay in the last coat, but when I go back into the booth after the clear has set and the booth is off, the top surface is peppered with these little dust things. The worst part is that when I try to sand them out, it only creates dimples around the dust specks. They actually feel like little spikes, because the clear adheres to them. I would appreciate any help... I'm about to lose my mind.

Sick of Re-Clears
Steve, Sacramento, CA

Steve: First, you're not alone—I've heard about this problem many times. Secondly, your problem is not dust, which means you could clean your booth til' you're blue in the face and it would make little difference. Let me take a wild guess—you live in a humid environment, and your compressor is pretty old and has outdated water traps. I'm saying this because you've described a condition that is caused by high humidity levels in the air line that supplies your spray gun. Everyone knows that humidity in the line can be even worse, and it can occur in a dry climate.

What's happening is that water moisture, which microencapsulated in the air, has not had a chance to condense out, so it's literally injected into your clear mixture through the spraying process. These sharp little "dust specks" you're talking about are actually crystals that are almost as tough as industrial diamonds—that's why they're so difficult to sand. It may look like dust has fallen, but those crystals are actually formed in the clearcoat as it sets and the tail solvents escape. The best way to eliminate these little suckers is to eliminate the in-line water vapor.

Normal water traps can only handle so much, so I recommend that you start by testing your lines. Get yourself a cheap electronic humidity gauge, from an electronics retailer (such as Radio Shack). Hold the probe in front of your air line, and let the air spray across it for approximately one minute. If the gauge indicates that your humidity is above 38%, it is not good (the ideal level is about 18%). The way to remedy this is to get yourself a new line and water trap.

VI. Mini Golf

The Front Nine:

i. The Castle
(under construction)

ii. The Waterfall
(under construction)

iii. The Crag—artificial rock climb
(under construction)

iv. The Oriental Pagoda
(under construction)

v. The Bumper Boat Pond
(under construction)

vi. The Clownface
(under construction)

vii. The Windmill
(under construction)

viii. The Jam-Bear-E
(under construction)

ix. The Snack Shack
(under construction)

The Back Nine:

The New Testament Holes:

In today's franchised brand character-choked mini golf industry, it's refreshing to see someone attempt a relatively unique theme. And what better brand of recognition than God's own time-tested characters and stories available for not a dime of trademark licensing?

Three white crosses loom near the parking lot and mark the final hole; to get there determined players putt their way through the hazards and miracles of the Good Book.

After renting a club and a ball in the gift shop, eager fans line up at hole #1, The Book Of Genesis. The first nine holes are inspired the Old Testament: Adam and Eve's Expulsion from the Garden, Moses parting the Red Sea, Daniel and the Lion.

We're amused that the scenes are comprised of repurposed lawn ornaments and cement statuettes—no priest-folk artist spent his life carvings here. Jonah sits in a whale's mouth, comfortable in shorts; a statue of St. Francis monitors porcelain animal pairs boarding the Ark.

The New Testament holes are sparsely decorated, looser, at least one featuring elves and men in lederhosen where an Apostle or leper might have done the trick.

An uphill challenge past the crosses finishes at the Lord's ascension up to Heaven.

VII. Convention Center (EXPOguide)

Booths 1-10

ACC Craftfair Baltimore
ACC Craftfair Columbus
ACC Craftfair San Francisco
Accessories-The Show
Accessories-The Show-Holiday Resort
ACCI International Craft Expo
ACCI International Craft Expo
ACE Hardware Spring Convention & Exhibit
ACE/Annual Claims Exposition & Conference
ACESS EXPO

Booths 11-23

AEC Web Expo
AEC Web Expo
AEF Automechhanika Istanbul
AEF Broadcast Cable & Satellite
AEF Industry
AEF Petroleum Istanbul
Aerosense/Aerospace Defense Sensing & Controls Symposium
Aerospace Congress & Exhibition
AESF SUR/FIN-Society of Electroplaters & Surface Finishers
AFCEA Infotech/Armed Forces Communications & Electronic Association
AFIA Expo/Feed Industries Show

Booths 24-32

AFRIBUILD
African Studies Association Show
AFRIWATER
Ag Expo Sioux Falls
Agri Farm Show
Agri News Farm Show
AGRO TECH India
AGROMEK/Agricultural Farm Show
AHR Int'l Air-Conditioning, Heating, Refrigeration Exposition

Air
Air & Waste Management Association Annual Meeting

Booths 39-54

Allied Sportsfishing Trade Convention
All-Ohio Safety & Health Congress & Exhibition
All-Ohio Safety & Health Congress and Exhibit
alt Lake Machine Tool & Manufacturing Expo
AM/FM Intl Conference (Automated Mapping/Facility Management)
Amarillo Home Show
AMBIENCE/Australia Furniture & Interior Design
Ambiente Arabia

Booths 66-79

Aircraft Interiors Conference
Airport China
Alabama Dental Association Annual Session
Alabama Food Service & Nutrition Expo
Alaska Hospitality & Foodservice Expo
Alaska Women's Shoes
Alberta Beauty Convention
Alberta Gift Show Spring
Alberta Pork Congress
Albuquerque Home & Remodeling Show
Alexander Graham Bell Association for the Deaf

VIII. The Goths

> *Being Goth, for me, is seeing beauty, and its coming destruction, at the same time. For me...it's the last dance as the walls are crumbling down around you.*

Being a Bad Kitty means that we may be domesticated, but we are not tame. Our claws are still the sharpness of a hunter, beneath our lounging sensuous forms is muscle. We can strike and strike hard, but only when we feel threatened, and we are always in control of the situation we are in. Bad Kitties kick ass, but take names beforehand.

Being a Bad Kitty means that we do what we want when we want. We cannot please everyone, so we might as well please ourselves. Being comfortable is always preferable to being "in". What we wear and what we enjoy is a part of our beings that we will not compromise. It is an expression of ourselves. We accept that it might mean we do not 100% fit in everywhere, but Bad Kitties enjoy their own territory anyway.

Being a Bad Kitty means making everyday acts sensuous. From bathing with lots of oils to eating t.v. dinners by candlelight, everything that we do can become a ritual to ourselves for us to enjoy and revel in, purring all the while. It is sitting in the sun, dozing. It is a single piece of Godiva chocolate. It is chai tea at just the right temperature. It is velvet leggings. It doesn't matter what is being done, as long as it is lengthy, drawn out to the utmost, and done with full sensual enjoyment.

Being a Bad Kitty means that there are going to be some people who cannot stand us, either because we are foreign to them, because our coat is the wrong shade, because we are shaped like a Maine Coon and not like a Sphinx. In true Bad Kitty fashion, ignore them. These people do not understand the true mystical nature of the Bad Kitty, and we cannot teach the ignorant. And if there is something a Bad Kitty is a master at, it is "ignoring with style".

Being a Bad Kitty means wearing what we want to wear, when we want to wear it, and everyone else can piss off. The only requirement is that it is as sensual as we are. We know what looks best on us, and we do not moan about those few extra pounds or the fact that perhaps our legs are just two inches two short. We are works of art, we know how to be sensuous at any size or shape or color of coat, and we play up with style. Bad Kitties are NEVER trashy.

Being a Bad Kitty means having groups of other Bad Kitties for social grooming and fun, but never taking on the group mind. Bad Kitties can associate with other Bad Kitties without the cat-fights and territorial battles, because that is undignified, and we would rather be a DOG for a day than be undignified. Bad Kitties do not feel the need to argue why we differ on certain points, and if we are truly with other Bad Kitties, explanations should be unnecessary anyway.

Being a Bad Kitty means remembering the Laws of Goth when appropriate, enjoying past pleasures and treats, but never resting on the past's laurels. There are always new territories to explore, new terrain to conquer, and new bad kitty things to do. Being a Bad Kitty means to never be bored.

Being a Bad Kitty means taking risks. Nine lives are built in, and rather lose one of those lives to experience than hoard them for a rainy day that never comes. Be as confident as a cat crossing the street. There are always a few people who are going to speed up and try to hit us, but as a Bad Kitty, we know how to swerve when we need to, and when to let that cat in front of us get hit by the car.

Being a Bad Kitty means that taking responsibility is a subtle art like anything else. Falling off the couch happens when we lick our fur back into place, and stalk away with dignity. Next time, we'll remember how to do things properly.

Most of all, being a Bad Kitty is KNOWING how beautiful and bad we really are...and loving every minute of it. Keep your coat sleek and neat, your claws well trimmed but sharp, keep yourself graceful and your tail up always. All Bad Kitties, no matter the size, breed, fur coloration or temperament, are works of art, and the people around them recognize it, even if they do not know why they are drawn to you, drawn they are.

IX. The Hermes Effect

look at yourself in the most critical fountain

don't decide any price in advance

don't try to impress the Eastern Bloc toilet attendant with your German

don't take the last five years and look at the figures and supply the fashionable curve of de facto on that

don't let it all hang out with a new sailor tattoo

don't placate badgers

so what if squirrels are eating out of your bird feeder

don't set up a vigilante eco-militant gloomsite just because your neighbor has

don't multi-purpose mosquito netting

don't expect any new results with the gentle cycle

my other car is… stolen

don't buy anything proudly brewed because it isn't

don't be stricken with blazer envy

don't decide to take a giant step forward and do your own thing

wear moccasins but call them dock-siders

one way to adopt a male attitude is by shelving a lot of feelings while in the kitchen

Grace, Ethan, Jake and Sparker… what's required is to SEE abuzz

wear white patent leather shoes to a thesis defense

don't give extra lip on the follow through

make yourself into an armored truck—worse days are coming

X. Popes (crossing the threshold of Hope)

i. Jesus

Christ is unique! Unlike Muhammad He does more than just promulgate principles of religious discipline to which all God's worshippers must conform. Christ is not simply a wise man as was Socrates, whose free acceptance of death in the name of truth nevertheless has a similarity with the sacrifice of the Cross. Less still is He similar to Buddha, with his denial of all that is created. Buddha is right when he does not see the possibility of human salvation in creation, but he is wrong when, for that reason, he denies that creation has any value for humanity. Christ does not do this, nor can he do this.

ii. The virtue of optimism

that becomes rooted in the human spirit would appear to be an essential requirement of our times in order to counter the current trends towards either arrogant triumphalism or pessimism or resignation. We must adopt an attitude of confidence based on personal commitment and optimism, willingness and perseverance by all responsible citizens.

iii. Men will surrender

to the spirit of the age. They will say that if they had lived in our day, faith would be simple and easy. But in their day, they will say, things are complex; the Church must be brought up to date and made meaningful to the day's problems. When the Church and the world are one, then those days are at hand.

iv. Falsehood

will characterize that class of men who will sit in judgment to pass sentence according to law: between the father and his son, litigations will subsist. The clergy of the holy church will be addicted to pride and injustice. Women will abandon feelings of delicacy, and cohabit with men out of wedlock.

v. Seven years

before the last day, the sea shall submerge Eirin [Ireland] in one inundation.

vi. Before the comet comes,

many nations, the good excepted, will be scourged by want and famine. The great nation in the ocean that is inhabited by people of different tribes and descent will be devastated by earthquake, storm, and tidal wave. It will be divided and, in great part, submerged. That nation will also have many misfortunes at sea and lose its colonies.

[After the] great Comet, the great nation will be devastated by earthquakes, storms, and great waves of water, causing much want and plagues. The ocean will also flood many other countries, so that all coastal cities will live in fear, with many destroyed.

All sea coast cities will be fearful, and many of them will be destroyed by tidal waves, and most living creatures will be killed, and even those who escape will die from a horrible disease. For in none of those cities does a person live according to the Laws of God.

vii. A powerful wind

will rise in the North, carrying heavy fog and the densest dust, and it will fill their throats and eyes so that they will cease their butchery and be stricken with a great fear.

viii. In the 20th century

there will be wars and fury that will last a long time; whole provinces shall be emptied of their inhabitants, and kingdoms shall be thrown into confusion. In many places the land shall be left untilled, and there shall be great slaughters of the upper class. The right hand of the world shall fear the left, and the north shall prevail over the south.

ix. When the great time will come,

in which mankind will face its last, hard trial, it will be foreshadowed by striking changes in nature. The alteration between cold and heat will become more intensive, storms will have more catastrophic effects, earthquakes will destroy great regions, and the seas will overflow many lowlands. Not all of it will be the result of natural causes, but mankind will penetrate into the bowels of the earth and will reach into the clouds, gambling with its own existence. Before the powers of destruction will succeed in their design, the universe will be thrown into disorder, and the age of iron will plunge into nothingness.

When nights will be filled with more intensive cold and days with heat, a new life will begin in nature. The heat means radiation from the earth, the cold the waning light of the sun. Only a few years more and you will become aware that sunlight has grown perceptibly weaker. When even your artificial light will cease to give service, the great event in the heavens will be near.

x. In the days of peace

that are to come after the desolation of revolutions and wars, before the end of the world, the Christians will become so lax in their religion that they will refuse to receive the Sacrament of Confirmation, saying, "It is an unnecessary Sacrament."

xi. The twentieth century will bring

death and destruction, apostasy from the Church, discord in families, cities and governments; it will be the century of three great wars with intervals of a few decades. They will become ever more devastating and bloody and will lay in ruins not only Germany, but finally all countries of East and West.

After a terrible defeat of Germany will follow the next great war. There will be no bread for people anymore and no fodder for animals. Poisonous clouds, manufactured by human hands, will sink down and exterminate everything. The human mind will be seized by insanity.

During this period, many men will abuse of the freedom of conscience conceded to them. It is of such men that Jude the Apostle spoke when he said, "These men blaspheme whatever they do not understand; and they corrupt whatever they know naturally as irrational animals do." They will ridicule Christian simplicity; they will call it folly and nonsense, but they will have the highest regard for advanced knowledge, and for the skill by which the axioms of law, the precepts of morality, the Holy Canons and religious dogmas are clouded by senseless questions and elaborate arguments.

xii. These are the evil times,

a century full of dangers and calamities. Heresy is everywhere, and the followers of heresy are in power almost everywhere. Heretics and tyrants will come suddenly and unexpectedly; they will break into the Church. They will enter Italy and lay Rome waste; they will burn down churches and destroy everything.

XI. Welcome to my Guest Book!

Name: Chad
Hometown: Sioux Falls
Sent: 11:27 PM 1/12

I agree with Harold—you have a GREAT site here.

Name: Michelle
Hometown: Detroit
Sent: 8:48 PM 1/11

Excellent!!! Glad to see you have Gladiators... I'm looking for Roman Infantry. Do you have any ideas? My grandfather used to paint miniatures. I'm looking to do the same but have no idea how to start. If you think you would like to help me... drop me a line.

Name: Coby
Hometown: Inverness
Sent: 11:51 PM 1/9

Your site is one of the most interesting I've seen on miniatures. I like it very much. Also the link to Elke's carpets make me very happy... I wish you all a lot of success and fun!!

Name: Mick
Hometown: Sydney
Sent: 11/30

How are you? Very good site, most impressed.

Name: Tim
Hometown: Aurora
Sent: 9:02 PM 11/9

Hi Pete (I already said hi to Kevin). Drop in and see us next time you're around this way. I'll put a link on my sites.

Name: Johni
Hometown: Iowa
Sent: 8:32 1/2

The fire places look great!

Name: Phil
Hometown: Brussels
Sent: 6:14 PM 12/26

Thanks for processing my order so promptly. Looking forward to receiving your figures. Will send you pics of my Crecy diorama when finished.

Name: Spencer
Hometown: Kenilworth NJ
Sent: 2:17 PM 9/23

Always interesting to find new sources for castings. Have submitted my first order. Look forward to reviewing Rosedale figures.

Name: Alan
Hometown: Lancaster
Sent: 01:30 PM 9/21

This is some of the coolest ive seen!!!

XII. Bubble Wrap

Sealed Air Corporation (NYSE:SEE) is a leading global manufacturer of protective and specialty packaging materials and systems. We offer a broad range of differentiated products to a diverse set of markets. Our products provide clear, measurable benefits and create value by solving our customers' problems. This strategy sets the stage that determines our culture, our activities and the economic profile of our business.

>   Investor Information
>   Company History
>   Code of Conduct
>   Career Opportunities
>   Packaging Laboratories
>   Environmental, Health & Safety Policy

OOOOOOOOOOOOOOOOOOOOOOOOOOOOOOOOOOOOOOOOOOOOOOOOOOOOOOOO

Our products provide superior package integrity (tougher and stronger), protect our customers' products during distribution, extend product shelf life, and provide shrink, clarity and gloss superior to other packaging materials for similar applications. They are primarily sold directly to our customers for:

>   fresh meat (chilled or boxed beef, pork, lamb, and veal)
>   smoked and processed meats
>   poultry
>   fish
>   cheese
>   produce
>   bakery
>   pumpable food
>   specialized medical end uses

OOOOOOOOOOOOOOOOOOOOOOOOOOOOOOOOOOOOOOOOOOOOOOOOOOOOOOO

Some rigid trays and absorbent pads are sold through distributors who are focused on serving grocers and food processors.

Sealed Air has developed strong relationships with our customers through the various distribution channels we employ to serve them. These relationships constitute strategic partnerships in which we work with our customers to help them achieve their business objectives.

Distribution Channels for Protective Packaging Products
Distribution Channels for Food Packaging Products

Sealed Air has over 1,200 field sales and technical support professionals worldwide, many of whom are food scientists or packaging specialists. This sales force represents our strong commitment to our customers. We are well positioned to find, sell to and service customers wherever they conduct their business, through our channels of distribution.

0000000000000000000000000000000000000000000000000000000

We are also well positioned to support product development and package design for our customers with over 30 food science and packaging application labs located around the globe.

Combining our labs with the expertise of our sales and development organizations, we employ our consultative selling approach to solve our customers' specific problems and to ensure that we meet the needs of each customer. This consultative selling approach provides the opportunity to sell and deliver the value of the solutions and services we provide.

Most of our products are part of a complete system solution to our customers' packaging needs. An equipment component of the solution is integrated into the packaging process and is necessary to produce the package that protects our customers' products. Both the material and equipment affect the integrity of the package and the efficiency of the packaging operation. Our equipment offering coupled with our expertise in equipment system design and integration position us to provide additional value to our customers.

XIII. Stadium Seating

There is no substitute for a comfortable seat with a great view of the screen. While all of the Starplex Cinema's theaters feature full-backed rocker chairs with armrest cupholders and loveseats, the Starplex Galaxy 16 also features the latest innovation in motion picture theater design—stadium seating in all sixteen auditoriums.

What is stadium seating? As you can see on the picture to the left, stadium seating means that the theater's rows of seating are arranged using a tiered system, making each row sixteen inches higher than the one in front of it. This means that your view of the screen will never be obscured by a taller patron in front of you with a Texas-sized hat or hairdo. Handicap seating is easily accessible on the entry level row. The auditoriums' surround sound fields have been specially aligned to conform to the unique auditory environment created by tiered seating, meaning you'll still enjoy an incredible digital sound experience while gaining a better view of the screen.

The Teddy

This seat was designed for comfort and a maintenance free life. With just two fixings and no assembly the price of this self-supporting seat is very economical. The unique drain allows water to flow off the seat and has internal reinforcing. Available in a variety of colours.

Teddy specification

* One-piece polypropylene moulding
* Integral plastic inserts over fixings

- Recess for seat numbering
- Smooth finish
- Ultra-violet stabiliser or flame retardant additives extra

The Lincoln

Mounted on a simple but sturdy metal underframe the Lincoln offers an economical method of seating with a modern design. Mild steel frames are of rigid construction and available in a choice of coatings. The polypropylene seat is available in a variety of colours.

Lincoln specification

- One-piece polypropylene moulding
- Recess for seat numbering
- Smooth finish
- Mild steel welded support frame
- Metalwork coated in LDPE
- Ultra-violet stabiliser or flame retardant additives extra

The Hampton

Our latest design for spectator seating has so many advantages. With both spectator and stadium maintenance in mind, this ergonomically designed seat was created to give excellent comfort as well as a maintenance free life. Having the benefit of just two fixings and no assembly the price of this self supporting seat outstrips any conventional tip-up seat. The unique drain allows water to flow off the seat without it draining under the seat itself, unlike other seats in its class. Due to its modular design they can be installed either in a straight or curved line and at any seat centre. In addition to a central recess for seat numbering, smooth finish and anatomical front, the whole seat has integral inner reinforcing.

Hampton specification

* One-piece polypropylene moulding with colour fastness of 7-8 on the blue wool scale, dependent on colour.
* Standard colours available - Black, White, Red, Green, Blue, Yellow.
* Integral plastic inserts over fixings
* Recess in back for seat numbering
* Variable seat centres
* Smooth finish
* Third optional fixing to front of seat
* Conforms to FIFA & UEFA regulations
* Passes strength test to level 5 of BS4875 Parts 1 & 3 - severe contract use

Extras

* Ultra-violet stabilised or flame retardant additives for polypropylene
* Fire retardant additive
* CAD layout and design service available
* Seat numbers, riveted-on aluminum or self-adhesive plastic
* Alternative material Nylon for greater durability and resilience
* Available in many colours to BS or RAL colour references
* Seat frames available to suit different terracing—see chart

The Restall Stadium Seating Collection

First installed in the early 1970s, Restall's tip-up seats have outsold and outlasted their competitors with over 2,000,000 sold worldwide. As you will see, our comprehensive range of seats gives a wide choice to suit any site condition.

Restall International Stadium Seats are installed at most English Football League and County Cricket Grounds and also many leading sports venues throughout the world. We have a variety of seat styles suitable for any stadium.

Restall International's spectator seating range have seats and backs in UV stabilised polypropylene for external use, available in a choice of colours. Support frames are mild steel with plastic coated finish. Galvanizing is available as self finish or prior to coating. Fixings are zinc plated and/or stainless steel. Accessories available are seat numbers, row end plaques, armrests and upholstery on certain models.

XIV. Rubber Ducks

Rubber Duck Alignment:

Side-By-Side Lineup

Made popular by the Radio City Rockettes, this method of lining up is best at promoting a risque attitude.

Single File Lineup

The most common alignment when people ponder having the ducks in a row. Great for the Karma!

Face-Off Lineup

The colors GREEN and MAUVE are complimentary, as are the fine sounds of bluegrass music.

Good Vs. Evil

This is a modification of the Face Off alignment and shows the classic conflict present in the universe.

Football Alignment

This alignment, based on the Face Off pattern, is extensively used in professional football circles. While this alignment requires more ducks, the end result is that more of your goals are completed and it fosters increased competitiveness.

The Huddle

Often associated with football, this alignment fosters cooperation and communication. Gregorian chants are compatible.

The Pool Rack

Ducks in formation always get their way. Often used in military air tactics, this alignment will augment your goals and produce fame and fortune.

The Circular Shuffle

This alignment has plenty of Ying and Yang and will go round and round for years without a problem. Use this alignment when you wish to foster a permanent loving relationship.

The Prisoner of War

This alignment is typically used to isolate and conquer the forces of evil. Whenever there is turmoil in your life, use this alignment for instant results.

XV. Senate

Because my client is an immigrant, do you think you might have a problem with that? Or that he was riding a bicycle? Are there other people in your family where there were personal injury cases involved? Any close friends or family as lawyers? Have you ever suffered a knee injury? Sports related injury? Have you ever known anyone who has suffered a knee injury? Do you use cabs? What's your feeling towards New York City cab drivers? What's your feeling towards people who bicycle in the city? Do you think bicycling in the city should be restricted to designated areas? Do you think cars, buses, should share the road with bicyclists? Do you ride a bike in New York City? Do you wear a helmet? Do you think there should be a law requiring bicyclists to wear helmets? Anything about that experience that I should worry about? Is your brother's case still pending? Is it fair to say that you work mostly as a personal trainer? How do you feel about the civic justice system in this country? The jury system? Do you feel, because your husband is a doctor, do you feel this could make you prejudice in any way? Do you think anyone who has gone this far, who has hired a lawyer and filed a suit, etc., should be awarded something? Does it bother you that an illegal alien can use our legal system and walk away with money even though he or she doesn't pay any taxes? Have you or anyone you've known been sued? Do you think that there is too much suing going on in this country?

2

•

THE

FALL

XVI. Senate

Do people sue each other too often in your opinion? What type of engineering work do you do? Do you own the apartment that you live in? Do you have any ill feelings toward landlords? Do you have any ill feeling toward commercial bus drivers? Do you have any feelings, or any ax to grind, with the Mobil Gas Company? Were you a resident of Texas at that time? Where are you finishing your MBA? Is she also from Texas? Do you have any feelings about commercial bus drivers? About the Greyhound bus company? Do you teach acting? Is that one of those financial counseling services for people in credit distress? How long have you worked with computers? When you were working as an engineer, what kind of work did you do? Did you compete as a professional tennis player? How long have you been a tennis instructor? In the States? Do you have any preconceived notions about the way businesses should be run? Do you have any feelings about the Mobil Gas Company? How do you feel about the civic trial system? Do you have any ill feelings toward commercial bus drivers? How would you describe your experience with commercial bus companies? How long have you taught American History? Do you have any problems, any ax to grind, with the Greyhound Bus Company? Mobil Gas Company? What field in American History do you teach? Do you teach the constitution, constitutional history? Are you presently suing someone? Are you being sued? Do you have any feelings about commercial bus drivers?

XVII. Rubber Ducks (For Sale)

Sunny Duck (beak color may vary)	$3.95
Glow in the Dark Sunny Duck	$3.95
Lifeguard Duck	$3.95
Hawaiian Duck	$3.95
Baby Duck	$3.95
Ball Player Duck	$3.95
Construction Duck	$3.95
Cowboy Duck	$3.95
Jester Duck	$3.95
Lady Duck	$3.95
Tropical Duck	$3.95
Duck on the Go	$.395
Original Duck	$3.95
Sailor Duck	$3.95
Snorkel Duck	$3.95
Scuba Duck	$3.95
Referee Duck	$3.95
Surfer Duck	$3.95
Captain Duck	$3.95
James Brown Duck	$3.95
Shakespeare Duck	$3.95
Hippie Duck	$3.95
Football & Cheerleader Duck	$3.95
Stars & Stripes Duck	$3.95
Space Shuttle Duck	$6.95
Uncle Sam Duck	$6.95
Dracula Duck	$6.95
Betty Boop Duck	$6.95
Santa Duck	$6.95
Queen Elizabeth Duck	$6.95
Groucho Marx Duck	$6.95
Blues Brothers Duck	$6.95
Babe Ruth Duck	$6.95
Mona Lisa Duck	$6.95
Beethoven Duck	$6.95
Carmen Miranda Duck	$6.95

XVIII. Stadium Seating (moneystory)

Tired of hitting the same old cinemas? Explore the possibilities this summer and give a few new and refurbished theaters a try.

It's 7 o'clock on a Saturday night, just a few minutes before the evening's features start, and a large line snakes through the lobby. Still, only two ticket sellers peer from behind a huge glass wall of ticket stations. Small annoyances like this detract from an otherwise enjoyable experience at City North 14. If you steer clear of the filthy restrooms, you'll enjoy the stadium seating with amazing sound systems and primo sight lines. A quality concession stand sells Uno's pizza, ice cream bonbons and chicken tenders, and a small video game area is well equipped for gaming connoisseurs. There's even a booth that will take your picture, record a voice message and email them both to a friend for $1.

Garage parking is convenient and reasonably priced at $2, but evening ticket prices ($9) can make an expensive night out for two after a trip to the concession stand.

Neat feature: A birthday party room for kids and a summer movie camp, featuring matinees like "Rugrats in Paris" and "The Grinch" for young viewers.

Ticket prices: $9 ($6 before 6 p.m.)
Food prices: (3 stars) (small popcorn, $2.75; small pop, $2.75)
Food quality: (3 stars)
Screen size: (4 stars)
Comfort: (4 stars)
Sight lines: (4 stars)
Parking: $2 (on-site garage)

*   *   *   *   *

Monolithic Cantera is a theatrical oasis. One wing of AMC Cantera 30 is steeped in a jungle motif, while the other is a trip through a cloud city. A theatrical oasis off I-88, the monolithic complex is surrounded by eateries such as Red Robin, Rock Bottom Brewery and Max & Erma's—ideal places for a bite before or after a show. Concession stands inside are standard with few surprises, but the condiment bars are elaborate and tidy.

As in most stadium theater seats, it's easy to lounge back on puffy headrests, placing your drink in convenient armchair cup-holders. Cantera 30 is a standard movie-going experience, with lots of free parking, quick ticket lines and quirky decor.

Neat feature: Tired of waiting in line for candy? Cantera has a couple of vending machines with the same candy that's sold at the concessions.

Ticket prices: $8.50 ($6.50 matinee)
Food prices: (small popcorn, $2.50; small pop, $2.50)
Food quality: (2 1/2 stars)
Screen size: (4 stars)
Comfort: (3 1/2 stars)
Sight lines: (4 stars)
Parking: free (on-site)

*   *   *   *   *

Evanston's movie hub exudes personality. What more could you ask for? When movie fans die, they'll want heaven to look like Century 12 & CineArts 6 in Evanston, two movie houses in one. Taking the best from smaller art house cinemas and stadium seating venues, Evanston's movie hub exudes style and personality. Excellent service and expansive theaters in the mainstream wing are a nice contrast to the smaller, more intimate theaters inside CineArts 6.

Even better, CineArts houses a full bar called The Rhythm Room (although alcohol is not allowed in the theaters), complete with a piano in one corner. You can even order cheesecake and take it in with you (delicious, minus stale whipped cream).

Food choices abound in Century 12 as well, from hand-scooped ice cream and shakes to Ben & Jerry's pints and bulk candy bins. Inside, the chairs are roomy, and you can even move the armrest up to snuggle with your sweetheart.

While area construction is confusing to navigate, free parking down the block can cap an otherwise stellar evening at the cinema.

Neat feature: Above the piano in The Rhythm Room are dozens of classic movie posters, some of them in foreign languages. Huge one-sheets from "Raging Bull," "Persona" and "Metropolis" reach to the vaulted ceiling.

Ticket prices: $8.75 ($5.50 before 6 p.m.)
Food prices: (2 1/2 stars) (small popcorn, $2.95; small pop, $2.95)
Food quality: (3 1/2 stars)
Screen size: (3 stars)
Comfort: (4 stars)
Sight lines: (4 stars)
Parking: free (down the block)

*   *   *   *   *

What this four-screen neighborhood cinema lacks in modern movie-going amenities, it makes up for with nostalgia and charm. Sure, the refurbished Davis in Lincoln Square may not have stadium seating or surround-sound speakers—and sometimes seeing a movie here is like listening to it through an AM radio. The isle carpets are frayed and movie trailers may be shown off-center and through the wrong lens—but where else can you buy handfuls of Boston Baked Beans and Runts for 25 cents through those old hand-cranked vending machines?

When buying tickets through what looks like a bank teller's window framed with stained glass, it's hard not to return the ticket seller's smile. Your smile will continue when you see the vintage publicity shots adorning the walls featuring John Wayne, Elizabeth Taylor and Bela Lugosi.

The Davis Theater, just off the Western Avenue L-stop on the Brown Line, is clean (three employees dash in after a feature to sweep up derelict popcorn containers) with an attentive, kind staff.

Neat feature: A long, tastefully lighted hallway serves as an art gallery, with work from local artists for sale.

Ticket prices: $7 ($5 matinee)
Food prices: (3 stars) (small popcorn, $2.25; small pop, $2.25)
Food quality: (2 1/2 stars)
Screen size: (2 1/2 stars)
Comfort: (2 stars)
Sight lines: (2 stars)
Parking: street

XIX. Bubble Wrap (Net Sales)

We derive roughly 40% of our net sales from our protective packaging products. These include:

> Instapak® foam-in-place packaging systems
> Korrvu® suspension and retention packaging
> Bubble Wrap® cushioning materials
> Cell-Aire® thin polyethylene foam
> CelluPlank™ and Stratocell™ foam plank
> Fill-Air™ inflatable packaging
> Jiffy™ protective mailers
> Trigon® security envelopes
> Cryovac® high-performance shrink films

We derive roughly 60% of our net sales from our food and specialty packaging products. These include:

> Cryovac® shrink bags
> non-shrink laminate materials
> shrink films sold for food end uses
> rigid trays
> absorbent pads

0000000000000000000000000000000000000000000000000000

We also design and sell packaging systems to facilitate the use of our products for our customers. These products provide superior protection against shock, abrasion, and vibration compared to other forms of packaging in similar applications.

In the case of Cryovac® shrink films, they provide superior shrink, toughness, clarity and gloss. These products are sold largely through industrial distribution to a diverse set of industrial end users.

XX. Welcome to my Guest Book! (My Freebies)

This section is all about me...
It is, and will remain, a work in progress...
Here you find links about me personally, my likes, my hobbies,
and especially my testimony.

My Garden

Not long ago I was trimming some trees

  In my backyard and I got stuck

    In the palm severely—

  It was very deep and hurt alot

As I looked and saw it bleeding I heard

  The word of the Lord say

This is a small idea of what I did for you

    And although he didn't cause that to happen

      He did speak to me

And teach me more about Himself

My Kittys

This is Slater our miracle cat.
He is a miracle because he was born to a stray mom and dad
And was only one of 3 brothers and sisters to survive
A cat's disease called distemper.
Have you ever taken your cat's IQ test?
Slater is in the top 5%!!!

This is Teddy.
We found him at an animal shelter.
At that time he had no fur.
Here's a picture of him with it all grown back.

This is Pouncey our first cat.
She is such a sweetheart.
She loves to sit with me while
I am at the computer.

My Freebies

There are always free books at the Billy Graham site.

Send Me a Note.
Let me know if you prayed with me.

XXI. Popes (Product Directory)

Plush Dolls/Bears   Nightlites   Plaques, Pictures & Wall Crosses   Patron Saint Items   Veils   Holy Bears   Deacon Stoles   Sports Minded Party Supplies   Copes   Processional Candles   Wedding Caketoppers   Choir Robes   Clerical Apparel   Marriage & Family Living   Spanish Titles Bells & Chimes   Pyxes & Burses   Ewer & Basin   Holy Water Sprinklers Palm for Palm Sunday   Ash for Ash Wednesday   Crown of Thorns Liturgical Desk Calendars   Kings' Tents & Accessories   Glitter Domes Smoky Mountain Pine   Douglas Fir   Sierra Fir   Stations of the Cross Visions of Mary   Visions of Our Lady   Infant of Prague   Grottos   Your Irish Dog   Parade Wear

XXII. The HERMES Effect: Partnership Concept

The HERMES Partnership, named after the son of Zeus who is delivering the messages of the Olympian gods,

is the network of leading independent telecom research centers in Europe. It brings together more than 500

highly skilled researchers from various disciplines. It can be considered a virtual center of competence

with a strong focus on wireless communications, including cellular systems, high speed local area networks,

satellite communications and positioning. Fields of experience cover applications and multi-media services,

network infrastructures, transmission techniques and system component implementations. The HERMES

partnership offers the following services: Inter-disciplinary contract research, technology watch, specialized training courses on emerging technologies, provision of evaluation infrastructure and technological consulting.

XXIII. The Goths (Fall Sale)

When these are gone, they really will be gone!

GAF-043 $10.99

Silver tube beads, cobalt blue seed beads, cobalt blue bicones and 3 wicked looking cobalt glass talons! Very icy looking, FRIGID, even ;)

GAF-044 $10.99

Gunmetal seed beads, ghost finished 4mm rounds, iridescent saturn beads and drops.† Cute little simple choker :)

GAF-045 $10.99

Perfect gothic rose choker... Center beads are genuine garnet rondelles. Others are black firepolish czech glass, garnet czech glass, silver tubes and rounds, and garnet seed beads... A tiny silver-plated rose graces the end of this choker.

GAF-046 $10.99

Itching for spring? Or just love amethyst? PERFECT!
Grass green seed beads, AB finished faceted green tubes, amethyst/white swirled rounds, and a centerpiece of genuine amethyst rondelles and one large amethyst round bead. Very cheerful (dunno what happened to me on this one, but I LOVE it! :)

GAF-047 $9.99

Another amethyst lover's choker! Amethyst seed beads and swirled amethyst/crystal bicones with AB finish crystal firepolish rounds, silver tube beads and little silver rounds. One glass amethyst drop at the center. Perfectly elegant! And... check out the little heart shaped padlock charm! Love it!!

GAF-048 $9.99

Hematite, gunmetal seedbeads and black crystal AB finish round glass beads. 5 tapered hematite pendants in the center. Silver-plated rose charm on one end. Preeettty.

GAF-049 $11.99

Yet another with amethyst :) This one is amethyst and garnet chips, separated by silver plated tube beads. Full of gemstones! Rose charm on one end of this one, too :)

GAF-050 $10.99

Fairy dust sparkles in the glass star in the center of this one! Clear AB finished hearts, rounds, and czech 4mm firepolish beads, silver lined seed beads, and tiny little silver-plated rounds. Of course, gotta have my little gothic rose hanging from one end :)

GAF-052 $14.99

Hard to scan this one so you can see how it works! It's a double wrap, the ends go in the front so you have the 2 red talons hanging on your throat :) Very cool! Black seed beads, czech firepolish glass in 4mm and 6mm, with 2 blood red vampire talons (becoming my signature? Very goth, verrrrry sexy :)

GAF-056 $16.99

Triple strand raver/party choker! This one has clear color lined acrylic beads in assorted sizes, assorted colors, with crystal seed beads. Measures 15 1/2 inches. This looks kinda blah in the pic, but it's sooooo colorful! Beauty, eh? :)

GAF-068 $18.99

Gorgeous red choker with wire dangles! Garnet glass seed beads, red e beads and red Indian glass rounds on the triple strand choker, with v shaped dangles in a very Victorian design. The dangles have red e beads, garnet glass 4mm faceted rounds, and red glass teardrops. On a triple strand hook and eye clasp, hand wrapped. Measures 15 inches. Gorgeous!

GAF-091 $12.99

Perfectly made for the Plus Size Goddess! The peacock black beads and silver compliment each other beautifully, and the beaded chains dangle gracefully. This one is substantial, the silver spacers in the dangles are solid metal (not silver). This one measures a little over 16 inches, and the weight of the dangles keeps it down from your neck a bit, to rest at the base of your throat. I'm glad the scanner picked up the oil slick type finish of these beads, but it's still much more impressive in person :)

XXIV. Convention Center

Booths 100-112

American Academy of Art Therapy National Convention
American Academy of Bovine Practitioners
American Academy of Dermatology Summer
American Academy of Homes & Services for the Aging
American Academy of Implant Dentistry

Booths 123-139

American Association of Managing General Agents
American Association of Petroleum Geologists Annual Convention
American Association of School Administrators Conference
American Association of School Administrators National Convention
American Association of Society Ball Expo Fall
American Association of Society Ball Expo Spring

Booths 200-210

American Bankers Association Convention
American Baseball Coaches Association
American Bus Marketplace
American Camping Association National Conference
American Ceramic Society
American College of Emergency Physicians
American College of Sports and Medicine
American College of Rheumotology Meeting

XXV. Mini Golf (*the money machines*)

1. PromiseLand

If you're thinking about the miniature (mini) golf business, let us help. We have forty years experience and have constructed over four hundred quality mini golf courses. We will gladly share any knowledge or information we have without cost or obligation. If you have questions about construction costs, timetables or just need general background information, give us a call today!

Miniature golf is coming of age! The new courses are outstandingly beautiful. Course design is much more creative—with lots of mounding and varying elevations accented by rippling streams, waterfalls and colorful landscaping. The game itself has become more challenging. And the number of players is increasing dramatically every year.

Miniature golf today is an inexpensive recreation the whole family can enjoy. Putting surfaces on new courses are designed to produce the same putting challenges found on regulation size greens—only in a miniature form. Subtle slopes in the greens, undulations and mounds have transformed miniature golf into a competitive, challenging game everyone can enjoy. Sand traps and water hazards come into play on many of the holes to add a whole new element of excitement.

Miniature golf has made this transformation without losing any of its fun. Young kids still love to play with Mom and Dad. The putting challenge enjoyed by older players doesn't affect the kid's fun one bit. They still whoop and holler and have a great time. Whether playing for score or just for laughs, everyone seems to love the new courses.

2. Wildwood, N.J.

To the casual player, they are miniature golf courses. To Rich and his clients, it's big business. He calls them *money machines*. "We build people money machines," he says. "But now, we're giving them instructions on how to print the money, too." These are not your father's miniature golf courses, built with 2- by-4s, fiberglass animals and creaky windmills.

These courses, which cost up to $750,000 to build, but average about $200,000, are made primarily of concrete and feature waterfalls, rock gardens, granite caves, planters, bushes, undulating greens—even roughs, just like real golf.

Harris' typical customer is a business owner who already runs a bowling alley, roller rink or go-cart track and wants to expand. Working with the company's two landscape architects, Lahey designs a multi-tiered course that takes best advantage of the site, with the most visible elements closest to the road, to attract players. "People come to us and many of them don't know anything about miniature golf," said landscape architect Glenn Lynn, vice president of Harris Miniature Golf.

Once design is complete, the company dispatches a six-man crew to do the building. Typically, they work 12-hour days and finish the course in about two weeks, Lahey said. Inevitably, the addition of miniature golf brings in new customers for the existing business and sends customers from the established business next door to try the golf, according to Lahey.

"I've heard it referred to as the perfect small business," said Lahey, 40, a Scranton, Pa. native who joined Harris as a salesman and ended up buying out the owner.

"Once you build it, there's not a lot to put back into it in the way of investment. The only expense is scorecards. You really need only one person to play per hour to pay your employee. If you have two, you're making money already."

When entrepreneur Keith Johnson set out to convert an alfalfa field in Rigby, Idaho, into a family fun park, he decided to look into miniature golf as one of its elements. He ended up hiring Harris to build an 18-hole course at The Riot Zone, which opened in June. "We were referred to them by other park owners and we were totally impressed. They worked so hard and so fast. And the course they built is like a little landscaped Mecca, with waterfalls and lakes and rivers and spray fountains. It's right next to the freeway and it draws so much attention," Johnson said.

Another recent success story is Atlantic City Miniature Golf, an 18-hole course on the Atlantic City boardwalk that charges players $5 during the day and $6 at night. The course, which opened May 25, is located at a Boardwalk plaza that city leaders had struggled to find a use for, trying an ice rink and then a small amusement park before miniature golf. "We're getting hundreds of players a day, about 80 percent of whom are gamblers," said co-owner David Greenspun. "People keep thanking me for it."

Lahey says the success of Harris Miniature Golf, Inc. has led to numerous opportunities to branch out into other kinds of construction. "Not interested," he says. "All we want to do is miniature golf."

XXVI. Airbrush: Order the Video

Yesterday when I got home from an airbrush class, my airbrush video I had ordered from Nails in the Real World had arrived.... popped it in and oh my goodness. I felt so angry. WHY? Because if I had received it BEFORE the airbrush class I took I could have saved $300.00 !!! Suddenly I felt renewed. I learned far more in the video than in the whole three days of the airbrush class...Terri gives wonderful little shortcuts and hints and explains in great detail... everything, and I mean everything you beginners need to know. It is the BEST I HAVE EVER SEEN. Terri's "Nails in the Real World" airbrush video is the best... So grab your checkbooks and start buying... you won't regret it.

Georgette, Florida

I have been a nail tech for 15 years and have been airbrushing for the past 5 1/2 years. Over the years, I have purchased 8 videos on airbrushing. Some I thought were pretty good and some I was disappointed in. When I saw the information about Terri's Video "Nails in the Real World" I thought I might as well add one more to my collection.

I have to say, Terri's video is the best video I've seen covering all aspects of airbrushing. She focuses on the art of airbrushing and not just one particular brand of equipment. Even though I'm a seasoned airbrush artist I picked up many ideas and hints from Terri's video. I highly recommend this to anyone who is considering airbrushing or has been airbrushing for some time. It is appropriate for all skill levels. I'm anxiously looking forward to the next video that Terri makes.

Janene, Nail Elegance, Shelby, Ohio

Terri delivers a fine video production on airbrushing. Her valuable knowledge of various manufacturers equipment allows her to bring to the nail technician a complete understanding of airbrush maintenance and application. This video will make airbrushing virtually trouble free. A must for those who already own an airbrush system or for those thinking about purchasing a system. A great addition to your education library.

Peter, Airbrush Educator, owner of Silk Road Salon, Worcester MA

XXVII. Maria (Rave Reviews)

"They're all grown up. And they'd rather act right than rude."
—*Tulsa World*

"Anyone who slam dunks a spoon into his soup or laughs with an open mouth of food won't win fans outside the gym though his behavior might cause a few onlookers to cry, 'foul.' Rules of etiquette can save the day."
—*Tulsa World*

"Mothers enroll their daughters in The Pretty As A Picture course to reinforce the importance of manners."
—*Sand Springs Leader*

"Getting kids to write 'thank-you' notes seems to rank with bathing and eating peas…except for the ways taught through the Pretty As A Picture course."
—*The Kansas City Star*

"The niceties of neckties and knives…etiquette classes smooth rough edges for young men."
—*Kansas City Star*

"Who's the boor that said good manners are out of style? It's OK to be polite. Pretty As A Picture is finding enthusiastic response among Midwestern parents."
—*The Sun Newspapers*

"Learning social skills as young children enables them to be confident as teens and then adults."
—*The Lenexa News*

"Self confidence is the most important thing girls will learn during the course."
—*The Sun City Times, New Orleans*

"Children have fun while learning to feel good about themselves. [The instructor] even calls their homes to see how her students answer the telephone."
—*Phoenix Star*

"A course in etiquette makes your child Pretty As A Picture."
—*Las Vegas Sun*

"In today's society, parents try to teach their children at home, but it's the influence of another voice that gets the message across."
—*The Daily Record, Pennsylvania*

"Girls learn how to be Pretty As A Picture. Program teaches arts of poise, manners and helps boosts kids self esteem. I notice that if I stand up straight, my friends start doing it."
—*Desert News*

"Girls, boys enjoy fine things while learning refinement. A different cup of tea—smartly dressed little girls and boys sitting around a small table with half-size tea cups and small plates that hold anything from petit fours to tiny pizzas."
—*The Commercial Appeal*

XXVIII. B9D (Marketing and Sales)

B9D Stands for Beyond 9 Dots

or "thinking outside the box"—the type of thinking that companies need as industries converge, consumer demands increase, and leading companies can learn from experiences, practices, and mistakes of companies in other related industries.

Marketing and Sales Consultant

> Former Director of Consultant Industry Marketing, Worldwide, for one of the top 3 computer companies in the world
>
> Former Marketing Director for consulting and Alliance Manager for two of the "big 6" consulting firms at one of the largest software companies in the world
>
> Consulted to Northern Telecom as part of the Perot-Nortel-IBM Team covering the U.S. and Canada
>
> Teaches and/or taught at Kellogg Graduate School of Management (Northwestern University) and the Graduate School of Business at DePaul University
>
> Teaches and consults for Motorola University
> Ph.D. in Mathematics from Northwestern University
> M.B.A. in Marketing from DePaul University

Market Convergence and B9D

Convergence is creating unprecedented opportunities for technology and telecommunications companies. Formerly discrete and separate industries, computer technology, telecommunications, and consumer electronics now are intersecting.

This shift—and this evolution—makes B9D a valuable strategic sales and marketing partner for today's high tech companies.

A Sampling of Clients

Here is a sampling of clients that B9D contractors have worked with:

> Amoco
> Assembled Circuits
> Avalon
> Bell Canada
> Bell Sygma Information Services, Canada
> Calgene, Davis, CA
> Fabrik Industries
> IMAS, St. Charles, IL
> Lucent Technologies
> Metamor, Chicago, IL
> Mindsight Communications
> Motorola
> Northern Telecom (Nortel), Rochester, NY
> ORA, Chatsworth, CA
> Sales Consultancy, Dallas, TX
> Siemens Telecom
> Sounding Board Magazine
> Stentor Resource Center
> Telephony Magazine
> Wireless Review Magazine
> Worldspace, Washington, DC

XXIX: Ship Décor (Odyssey Special)

Public Rooms:

If you like Italian modern decor (as I do),
you'll love this ship. Throughout

the ship is a $20 million art collection
with sculpture, painting and stunning murals.

Public areas are decorated with warm wood
paneling accented with blue and green and white

marble floors (this can be slippery in the spa/fitness area).
All roads lead to the Piazza Italia Grand Bar,

with cushy sofas, small brass tables, wicker chairs,
a dance floor with live music and a bar with cocktails

and cappuccino. Like the center of a small Italian town,
it is lively throughout the day and a great place just to hang out

and people-watch. Directly off the Piazza Italia
is the Opera Showroom, a two-level lounge

reminiscent of a Greek amphitheater. I found sight
lines poor due to columns and seating that wasn't

particularly comfortable. Descending a wide staircase
from the Piazza you'll find Romeo Pizzeria,

with excellent thin-crust Italian pizza served
during the early evening and late at night,

plus the lovely Juliet Coffee Bar, with comfortable red
and white cushioned wicker couches and chairs.

The Via Condetti shopping area has several stores and
the European-style Excelsior casino, with tiled Mosaic

walls, has the full range of slots and gaming tables.
The Diva Disco, situated atop the ship with 360-degree windows,

has great views by day but poor acoustics during disco hours.
I avoided the area because of the reverberating

sound that bounced off walls—the noise coupled with Italian
rap music did not make this my pick for the top ten discos at sea.

XXX. Guide 1-99

Since early last century, this city has been celebrated as the most beautiful city in this country. Taking its name from the meadow where the ancient settlement's great market used to be held, this city has long been a commercial success, and is now the third largest city in this region. The provincial capital of this city is one of the least visited cities in this country. The manufacturing town of this city, purveyor of glass and raincoats to the nation, is a major junction of rail and road routes. Since the beginning of the age of the tourist brochure, this city has been known for just one thing. This island is an island in the old sense: unspoiled with just a couple of hotels and one road that links the small part of the town to the old town on the hill. This city is sited high above the bus and train terminals. This town figures large on the map but is disappointing in actuality. This town sits perched on top of a sugarloaf hill, its position and surrounding countryside the nicest for some distance around. This town is named for the triangular expanse between wild, sparse land that rises between this valley and this river. You won't lack for diversions in this mountainous capital. For years the retreat of the wintering wealthy, this seaside town now enjoys a broad base of tourism. This fashionable resort is your best center for exploring this snowy string of mountains. This port is bustling with the comings and goings of hundreds of visitors.

EDGE BOOKS

INTEGRITY & DRAMATIC LIFE Anselm Berrigan $10
THEY BEAT ME OVER THE HEAD WITH A SACK Anselm Berrigan $4
ZERO STAR HOTEL Anselm Berrigan $14
COMP. Kevin Davies $12.50
AMERICAN WHATEVER Tim Davis $12.50
THE JULIA SET Jean Donnelly $4
MARIJUANA SOFTDRINK Buck Downs $11
METROPOLIS 16-20 Rob Fitterman $5
DOVECOTE Heather Fuller $10
PERHAPS THIS IS A RESCUE FANTASY Heather Fuller $10
SIGHT Lyn Hejinian and Leslie Scalapino $12
LATE JULY Gretchen Johnson $3
ASBESTOS Wayne Kline $6
THE SENSE RECORD Jennifer Moxley $12.50
STEPPING RAZOR A.L. Nielson $9
ACE Tom Raworth $10
ERRATA 5UITE Joan Retallack $12
DOGS Phyllis Rosenzweig $5
INTERVAL Kaia Sand $10
ON YOUR KNEES, CITIZEN: A COLLECTION OF "PRAYERS" FOR THE "PUBLIC" [SCHOOLS] Rod Smith, Lee Ann Brown, Mark Wallace, eds. $6
CROW Rod Smith, Leslie Bumstead, eds. $6
CUSPS Chris Stroffolino $2.50
HAZE: ESSAYS POEMS PROSE Mark Wallace $12.50
NOTHING HAPPENED AND BESIDES I WASN'T THERE Mark Wallace $9.50

AERIAL MAGAZINE
(edited by Rod Smith)

Aerial 10: LYN HEJINIAN co-edited by Jen Hofer *forthcoming 2005*
Aerial 9: BRUCE ANDREWS $15
Aerial 8: BARRETT WATTEN $16
Aerial 6/7: FEATURING JOHN CAGE $15

Books published by Aerial/Edge are available through Small Press Distribution (www.spdbooks.org; 1-800-869-7553; orders@spdbooks.org) or from the publisher at PO Box 25642 * Georgetown Station * Washington, DC 20007. When ordering from Aerial/Edge directly, add $1 postage for individual titles. Two or more titles postpaid. For more information please visit our website at www.aerialedge.com.